Intonation in Context
Teacher's Book

Intonation in Context

Intonation practice for upper-intermediate and advanced learners of English

Teacher's Book

Barbara Bradford

Advisory Editor: David Brazil

CAMBRIDGE
UNIVERSITY PRESS

PUBLISHED BY THE PRESS SYNDICATE OF THE UNIVERSITY OF CAMBRIDGE
The Pitt Building, Trumpington Street, Cambridge, United Kingdom

CAMBRIDGE UNIVERSITY PRESS
The Edinburgh Building, Cambridge CB2 2RU, UK   http://www.cup.cam.ac.uk
40 West 20th Street, New York, NY 10011–4211, USA   http://www.cup.org
10 Stamford Road, Oakleigh, Melbourne 3166, Australia
Ruiz de Alarcón 13, 28014 Madrid, Spain

First published 1988
Seventh printing 1999

Printed in the United Kingdom at J W Arrowsmith Ltd, Bristol

A catalogue for this book is available from the British Library

ISBN 0 521 31915 3 Teacher's Book
ISBN 0 521 31914 5 Student's Book
ISBN 0 521 26490 1 Class Cassette Set

Contents

Acknowledgements

I should like to thank:

– David Brazil, my advisory editor, whose work at Birmingham University inspired the development of this material. It has been necessary, however, to simplify his description of the system of intonation and to make some adaptations in presenting it here for teaching purposes. I take full responsibility for these simplifications and adaptations.

– The many students who have worked with the material in its various stages of development.

– The teachers and institutions who worked with the pilot edition and whose comments were so valuable in the production of the final edition.

– Studio AVP for producing the recordings, which are central to the course.

– The Phonetics Department at the School of Oriental and African Studies, London University, for assistance in obtaining the intonation contour displays.

– My family and close friends for their support and enthusiasm throughout.

– Finally, my editors, Christine Cairns and Jeanne McCarten, and Alison Silver, who edited the typescript.

BB

Introduction

Who is this course for?

Intonation in Context aims to help learners of English to perceive the system of intonation used by native speakers and ultimately to incorporate the system into their own performance.

It is designed to be used with upper-intermediate and advanced learners, as a supplement to a communicative coursebook. Learners who have reached a comparatively high level of proficiency in other aspects of English all too often seem to reach a plateau in their oral ability. There is, accordingly, no separate presentation of lexis or grammar in this course; it concentrates exclusively on the perception and practice of the system of intonation.

Intonation in Context is designed with two main groups of learners in mind: those working in groups with a teacher, with classroom listening facilities or a language laboratory, and those studying privately, with the use of a cassette recorder.

Basic problems in teaching intonation

There are at least three main problems in teaching intonation and in designing materials for the purpose.

First, intonation is an aspect of language not usually brought to the level of consciousness. In the speech of native speakers intonation patterns are planned at a deeply subconscious level, the units and contours being mapped out in the speaker's mind before he/she decides which words he/she will use. It is, therefore, intrinsically difficult to make a learner manipulate intonation *consciously* without running the risk of destroying the naturalness of his/her speech. Yet, if we are to help learners to avoid giving the kind of faulty signals which lead to social as well as linguistic misunderstanding, we need to give some training in the perception and imitation of models. By encouraging the learners to concentrate on the contextualised meaning and function of messages the course minimises the risk involved.

Secondly, intonation is fleeting and, therefore, inherently difficult to analyse. Native speakers respond intuitively to the intonation used by other native speakers. Foreign learners may need to discuss this seemingly complex phenomenon, and we must, therefore, find some way of enabling the learner to capture the fleeting moment and analyse it. Furthermore, in order to discuss intonation, we need access to a descriptive system which provides the necessary labels by which to refer to its parts. Then the learner will be able to discuss and come to understand what he/she is seeking to build into his/her own communicative competence.

Thirdly, there is the question of how to represent intonation on the printed page and, further, whether or not we should seek to represent all the phonetic detail. *Intonation in Context* attempts to represent only the meaningful (phonological) contrasts and adopts a simple method of transcription. The symbols have to be explained and understood from the outset and, although no claim is made that they are better than any other method of transcription, they represent a finite set of meaning contrasts and are eminently learnable. Thus, with this simple but comprehensive method of transcription, the learners have an analytical tool which they can use independently for discussion and study purposes.

The theory

Earlier approaches to the teaching of intonation have related it either to grammatical features or to attitudes. This course excludes all such attempts, and, in contrast, takes as its base a description of intonation which is derived from a study of the pragmatic use of linguistic forms to convey meanings in spoken discourse.

Intonation in Context is based on the descriptive system presented by David Brazil (1978, 1980 and 1985), which views intonation primarily as a feature of discourse and the developing interaction between speakers. Throughout the course intonation is demonstrated as an aspect of spoken language which is used systematically and which fundamentally affects the meaning of utterances and their function in conversation.

Brazil's description of intonation presents a system which itself is very simple. Yet, because it is finite, it enables us to account for all the choices that speakers make when they select the *forms* of intonation which will convey the meanings they intend. These choices can be seen to take into account the contextual features of the conversation.

The system has been slightly adapted here and, therefore, the material in the Student's Book does not cover the whole of Brazil's theory (Brazil, 1985). The features which were selected were those found to be the most frequently occurring in conversation and the most teachable. However, as a result of this selection, some important features have necessarily been omitted.

The eight units of the Student's Book cover the main communicative functions of intonation. Speakers realise these functions by selecting from options within the three components of the system: prominence, tone and key. Native speakers are able to use these three sub-systems simultaneously, but they are treated separately in this course for the purposes of teaching one feature at a time.

Prominence is the element of intonation which determines the 'noticeability' of words. A speaker makes a word more noticeable by making the accented syllable of that word stand out more than others in the context. This is achieved by making systematic use of such phonetic variables as vowel lengthening, increased volume and pitch variation.

The result is that certain stressed words in an utterance have a further degree of emphasis and become the focus of the hearer's attention. A speaker chooses to focus on these words because they carry the information which is most crucial in the message being conveyed. To illustrate this we might think of speakers on a bad telephone line. The words they would emphasise – mainly by increasing the volume – are those they would make prominent in a conversation in more normal circumstances.

Tone is used in this course to mean the rapid gliding movement of pitch which begins, and is often completed, on a prominent syllable (tonic). Three tones: the rise, the fall and the fall-rise have been selected here as the most frequently occurring in conversation. Each tone has a particular communicative value, and a speaker's choice of one rather than another has significance in the developing conversation.

Key refers to the relative pitch levels of utterances or parts of utterances. By sometimes raising or lowering small chunks (tone units) of what they say, speakers convey some aspect of meaning.

Brazil's theory also provides us with the descriptive labels which are needed in order for teachers and learners to be able to talk about intonation. They are listed and explained in a simple glossary on page 9 of this book. Please note that learners are not required to perceive or explain all the parts of the system represented by these terms.

Structure of the Student's Book

The Student's Book presents intonation as a system; the component features are dealt with one at a time. The book has eight units:

Unit 1 Highlighting

This unit is about prominence and the decisions a speaker makes in distributing prominence to give an utterance its intended meaning. By assigning a prominent syllable to a certain word (at a particular point in the developing conversation) the speaker foregrounds or 'highlights' that word. Decisions to highlight the selected words are influenced by the conversational context.

e.g. Did you take your motorbike?   NO. I HIRED a motorbike.
     Did you hire a car?   NO. I hired a MOtorbike.

Word accent and prominence   A prominent syllable is always an accented syllable of a word, but the converse does not apply. So, any accented syllable could become prominent if the speaker chooses to highlight the word containing it. The syllables *hired* and *mo* of motorbike will always have word accent in the above examples, but whether either or both of them also has prominence will depend on the context.

Unit 2 Telling and referring

This is the first of three units which demonstrate the use and meaning of tone. It introduces the simple distinction between the two types of tone – finally falling and finally rising – and selects the most frequently occurring of each type – the fall and fall-rise. The distinction can be simply explained in this way: when speakers choose to present what they say in any part of an utterance as new for their hearers they choose a falling tone.

If, on the other hand, they present what they say as already common ground between them at that point in the conversation, they choose a fall-rise:

e.g.   A: Can you tell me when the last bus leaves, please?
       B: // ∨↗ Well toDAY's SUNday // ↘ so it left an HOUR ago //

Unit 3 More telling and referring

This second unit on tone concentrates on the fall and fall-rise tones again but extends the work of Unit 2, requiring the students to manipulate longer pieces of discourse.

Unit 4 Revision and practice

This unit reactivates and consolidates what has been learnt in Units 1–3. The exercises are designed to give further practice in the perception and use of prominence and the two tones (↘ and ∨↗), and can be used by students requiring 'remedial' work or by those who are keen to make further progress and gain greater self-confidence.

The selection of activities includes some for recognition of the features: ear training and discrimination exercises, and analysis of dialogues. It also includes production activities, some tightly controlled, some less controlled, and some which combine the features which have been learnt.

Unit 5   Roles and status of speakers

This third unit on tone introduces the distinction between the two finally-rising tones (↗ and ↘↗) and the notion of conversational dominance. In discourse where the speakers have unequal status by virtue of their roles, occupations, etc., the dominant speaker may choose to reflect his/her status by using the ↗ instead of the more frequent ↘↗. In conversations between 'equals' one speaker may establish temporary dominance over the other by choosing to use the ↗ tone.

e.g.   Lisa: // ↘ But TOny // ↗ surely you REALised //
       // ↘ You OUGHT to have known BETTer //

Unit 6   Low Key information

This is the first of two units which demonstrate the sub-system of intonation which we call key. The use of Low Key, i.e. a drop of pitch level from mid to low on the first prominent syllable of a tone unit, marks that part of what is said as being in some way equivalent in meaning to what was said just before (or sometimes what is said immediately after).

e.g. // Only a couple of WEEKS ago // at the be_{GINNing of the MONTH} //

Unit 7   Contrasts

This is the second of the units demonstrating key: High Key. The use of High Key involves a move up in pitch level from mid to high on the first prominent syllable of a tone unit. High Key marks what is said at that point in the conversation as being in some way contrary to the expectations of the hearer(s).

e.g. John: // But you didn't LIsten //

     Tony: // Yes I ^{DID} //

Unit 8   Revision and practice

This unit revises, practises and consolidates everything that has been covered in the course. There are recognition, production and development activities of a similar kind to those in Unit 4.

Structure of the units

Each of Units 1–3 and 5–7 is divided into five sections and follows a standard pattern which represents a progression from receptive to productive activities:

1   Sensitisation

A particular feature of intonation is demonstrated in context. By means of questions and tasks the students have to recognise and discuss the use of the feature. The purpose of this section is to make the students aware of its communicative value.

2   Explanation

The significance of the feature and its communicative value are explained using examples from section 1. Where possible spectrographs showing the intonation contours of the example utterances, which have been heard in context, are displayed here.

3   Imitation

This involves the simple repetition of models derived from section 1 to encourage the students to produce the feature with accuracy and confidence. The section is kept short but the items can be repeated as often as is necessary.

4   Practice activities

These include a variety of activities which provide practice in recognition, discrimination and production. Where it is appropriate, answers are provided in the Teacher's Book.

5   Communication activity

The activity is designed for pair work and is based on an information gap between the students. Each activity has been designed to exploit the feature which has formed the focus of the unit. However, the full range of intonational features will come into play, so teachers should try to ensure at some stage that the focus feature is used appropriately.

Using the course

The course contains the Student's Book, the Teacher's Book and a cassette. It is designed to be used alongside a coursebook, ideally in lessons timetabled exclusively for intonation work. It is suitable for students working in a group or for students working alone.

The teaching notes which accompany each unit indicate the ways in which the material can be used in a class. They also contain the transcripts and answers to exercises, and it is therefore necessary for a student working alone to have the Teacher's Book. The notes which follow outline the approach and procedures.

The approach is
a) incremental: that is to say, the whole system of intonation is built up step by step. It is suggested, therefore, that the units are worked through in the order 1 to 8. Similarly, the sequence of the sections in each unit is designed to be worked through from section 1 to section 5. In some cases it may be necessary to leave out parts of sections, or you may wish to return to some parts for reworking, but the sections should initially be tackled in the order in which they are presented.
b) inductive: that is to say, the tasks and activities enable the students to acquire the rules underlying the practical use of intonation. As a consequence of this feature of the course, time must be allowed for valuable discussion and drawing conclusions.

Time   Each unit contains material for a lesson of about 50 minutes. If time is limited, or if students experience difficulty with any part of the units, the work should not be skimped or rushed. It is preferable to work on shorter stretches of the material – if possible at frequent intervals. In this case, what has been said about working through the sections of a unit in sequence should be kept in mind.

The revision and practice units offer flexibility of use; you can work through the activities as they are presented or you can select the ones which are most appropriate to your students' needs and interests.

Omissions have been necessary in adapting Brazil's description of the system for teaching purposes. A regrettably necessary omission is the feature Brazil calls *Termination*. This relates to the significance of the choice of pitch level at the tonic syllable and has a very important function in shaping discourse. This omission has meant that tonic syllables in the transcriptions are usually represented as being at the same pitch level as the onset of the same tone unit.

Transcription Unfamiliar transcription conventions have been kept to a minimum. Throughout the course prominent syllables are indicated by using small capital letters. Full-sized capital letters have been used for the personal pronoun 'I', when it is non-prominent, and for the initial letter of sentences and of names. Full stops and other punctuation marks have frequently been left out of transcriptions.

Glossary

TONE UNIT

This is a division of natural speech which corresponds to the speaker's organisation of what is said into units of information. Each tone unit has a single pitch movement. There is no direct relationship between the tone unit and any grammatical or discourse unit.

Transcription Tone unit boundaries are indicated by the use of two parallel lines: //

PROMINENT SYLLABLE

The tone unit will have, as a minimum requirement, one prominent syllable. It may have two, but very rarely more. The distribution of prominence is relative to the communicative value of the word (sometimes the syllable) at that point in the developing discourse. Thus, by assigning a prominent syllable to it, the speaker marks it as significant:

Transcription Prominent syllables are written in small capital letters.
e.g. // TURN slightly toWARDS me //

ONSET

The first prominent syllable of a tone unit.

TONIC SYLLABLE

The tonic syllable is the minimum element, the defining characteristic, of the tone unit. It is the place where the major pitch movement begins, and marks the focal point of the message. If there is only one prominent syllable in a tone unit, it is also tonic. If there are more, the last one is tonic.

Transcription Tonic syllables are written in small capital letters and underlined.
e.g. // TURN slightly to<u>WARDS</u> me //

TONES

The pitch movement that begins at a tonic syllable is called a tone. There are two broad classes of tone: those which finally fall (proclaiming), and those which finally rise (referring). This binary system represents the main meaning contrast, each of the tones having a particular communicative value.

Transcription An arrow indicating the direction of the pitch movement which begins at the next tonic syllable is placed at the beginning of the tone unit.

e.g. // ↘ TURN slightly to<u>WARDS</u> me //

KEY

This system operates between successive tone units, and involves the varying of the pitch level beginning at the onset, compared to the preceding tone unit. For any speaker there is a 'normal' pitch level, easily perceived by interlocutors, which Brazil calls 'mid'. The raising of this level is called High Key, the lowering of it Low Key.

Transcription Vertical arrows indicate the raising or lowering of pitch level at the onset.

e.g. Low Key: YES // to a ↓ LARGE ex<u>TENT</u> // it ↑ IS

High Key: // I ↑ THOUGHT you were in <u>PA</u>ris //

References

Brazil, D., *Discourse Intonation II*, University of Birmingham, Discourse Analysis Monographs No. 2, 1978.

Brazil, D., *The Communicative Value of Intonation in English*, University of Birmingham, English Language Research, 1985.

Brazil, D., Coulthard, R. M. & Johns, C., *Discourse Intonation and Language Teaching*, Longman, 1980.

Unit 1 Highlighting

The title

Discuss the meaning of 'to highlight' as it is generally used. Students may know of its use in different contexts, e.g. painting. It can be loosely explained as meaning 'to focus on', 'to draw attention to' or 'to accentuate'.

1 Sensitisation

1.1 Get the students to read the questions as a purpose for listening. They are intended as stimuli for discussion; encourage the students to talk about the situational context – the relationship of Alan and Louise, where the action is taking place, etc.

ANSWERS
i)   He is trying to take a photograph of Louise.
ii) Because he wants to get everything just right: the light, the position, Louise's expression, etc.
iii) Louise is very impatient and intolerant of Alan's fuss. She would prefer a snapshot approach.

1.2 This short extract will seem rapid, so play it as often as the students want. You may want to give them some guidance if they lack confidence. Tell them that there will be one or two words in each line which should be boxed.

ANSWERS
Alan: Turn slightly towards me.

         Your head slightly towards me.

Louise: Right?

Alan: No – only slightly towards me.

In each case the speaker highlights the words which he/she wants the hearer to notice at that point in the conversation. At one point

a word is very informative and at another point the same word is
less so.

1.3 As you play the conversation through again, break it into sections
so that the students have time to write down the examples they
hear. Repeat if you wish.

ANSWERS

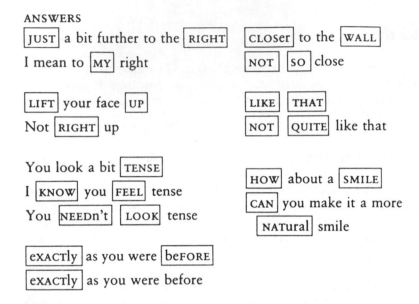

JUST a bit further to the RIGHT   CLOSer to the WALL
I mean to MY right   NOT SO close

LIFT your face UP   LIKE THAT
Not RIGHT up   NOT QUITE like that

You look a bit TENSE
I KNOW you FEEL tense   HOW about a SMILE
You NEEDn't LOOK tense   CAN you make it a more
                                      NATural smile

exACTly as you were beFORE
exACTly as you were before

2 Explanation

2.1 Go through the explanation with the students to make sure they are
confident that they understand.

2.2 The idea of prominence is introduced here. Check that the students
are clear that we talk about prominent syllables and highlighted
words.
   Note: Prominence is not just a matter of increased volume: it is,
in fact, a combination of features, one of them being a raised level
of pitch.

2.3 Draw attention to the transcription conventions – they will be used
from this point on.

3 Imitation

Whatever listening facilities you are using, try to check each student.

It is usually more difficult for learners to make words non-prominent than to make them prominent. This is not solely a matter of lowering the volume. A suggestion to 'hurry over' non-prominent words will help with this problem. Some revision of 'weak forms' would be appropriate, either as preparation or follow up. Weak forms are those words which in connected speech change their pronunciation, most usually by changing the vowel, e.g. am, have, some, can, etc. Whether or not such a word is used in its strong or weak form depends on its function in the utterance. Tell the students that the weak form will be used when the word is non-prominent.

e.g. aɪl ˈhæv səm suːp   *have* is prominent here

aɪl həv səm ˈsuːp   *have* is non-prominent here

some is non-prominent in both cases

4 Practice activities

4.1 This first activity is basically practice in recognition, but it can also be developed into a production exercise if students feel confident and if time allows.

Ask students to box the highlighted word in each utterance and then decide, perhaps with a partner, which of the questions provides the context; *or* ask students to tick the appropriate question in response to each utterance.

Then ask them to read the short dialogues, with student A producing the alternative version of the question and student B responding appropriately. (You could also ask them to test each other in pairs.)

ANSWERS
i) They hired a CAR   (b)
ii) No, the TRAIN was delayed   (b)
iii) The bank's on the CORNer   (a)
iv) I sent him a LETTer   (b)
v) It's next TUESday   (a)

4.2 Remind students to listen to the complete demonstration dialogue the first time and to repeat B's part the second time.

If the students are working in pairs, get them to listen to the recording, preferably after each dialogue. They should try to assess their own performance, and improve it if necessary and if they can.

ANSWERS

Model   B: I had CHICKen SOUP.
          B: CHRIS had toMAto soup and JAMES had tomato sAlad.

i) B: I had APPle PIE.
    B: CHRIS had CHERRY pie and JAMES had cherry CAKE.

ii) B: YES. It's the THIRty-FIRST.
    B: YES. SArah's is the TWENty-first and JENny's is the twenty-FOURTH.

iii) B: At the BACK ENtrance.
    B: At the MAIN entrance, which is right on the main STREET.

iv) B: I went LAST YEAR.
    B: YES. I'm going again THIS year. In fact, I'm going this MONTH.

v) B: She's got BLACK SHOES.
    B: She needed WHITE shoes to go with her white DRESS.

4.3 This activity is production practice and is very suitable for pair work, the students taking it in turns to be A and B.

Alternatively it can be used for class or individual work, which gives you a better chance to monitor some parts which the students may find difficult.

You can use the example as practice material, getting the students to repeat each of B's responses in sequence.

Tell the students that the five parts of the activity do *not* form a continuous dialogue.

The 'yes' and 'no' in brackets in (i), (iii), (iv) and (v) are not necessary for all the responses. In (v) the 'yes' is used in the second response and the 'no' in the third.

ANSWERS

i) B: It's the TWENty-FIRST.
    B: NO. It's the TWENty-first.
    B: NO. The twenty-FIRST.

ii) B: I've GOT a TICKet.
    B: I've got a TICKet.
    B: I've GOT a ticket.

iii) B: She SELLS CLOTHES.
    B: She sells CLOTHES.
    B: NO. She SELLS clothes.

iv) B: He's GOT a COLD.
    B: He's GOT a cold.
    B: NO. He's got a COLD.

v) B: We're not going till THURSday NIGHT.
   B: YES. We're not going till Thursday NIGHT.
   B: NO. We're not going till THURSday night.

4.4 Ideally, students work in pairs alternating roles. Get them to record themselves if possible and compare their own recording with the model.

The students should be able to do this activity quite quickly and without much conscious thought about the 'highlighting'. So, get them to work for fluency and expression.

ANSWERS

i) B: He's got a new CAR.
  B: He's GOT a new car.

ii) B: I've GOT some flowers.
   B: I've got some FLOWers.

iii) B: I've BEEN to Paris.
    B: I've been to PARis.

iv) B: Then I'll have some SOUP.
    B: Then I'll HAVE some soup.

v) B: He SAID he'd phone.
  B: He said he'd PHONE.

5 Communication activity

Check that the students understand the instructions.

Select any vocabulary from student B's menu which you think will be new for them, and introduce/explain it to the class.

The activity is designed to produce exchanges which involve words being used with and without prominent syllables, e.g.
B: Are you ready to order?
A: Yes.
B: What would you like to start with?
A: I'd like SOUP, please. What sort do you have?

B: There's toMAto, VEGetable or MUSHroom.
A: I'll have MUSHroom soup, please.
B: And for the main course?

This is a free activity to some extent. But try to make sure students are able to avoid making mistakes such as:
B: There's toMAto, VEGetable or MUSHroom.
A: I'd like MUSHroom SOUP, please.

Unit 2 Telling and referring

The title

First get the students to discuss the meanings of 'to tell' and 'to refer' and encourage them to explain the difference. Draw out the main point that 'to refer' is used when we assume some kind of familiarity on the hearer/reader's part with the information. In contrast, 'to tell' implies that the hearer/reader's knowledge or experience is being extended by the information.

1 Sensitisation

1.1 Play the recording and let the students just listen to this short exchange.

1.2 Play the recording as often as the students require.

ANSWERS

i) It falls. The pitch movement begins on 'give' and continues to fall through 'Claire'.

ii) Yes. Dave does not make 'Claire' prominent here, which suggests that he does not need to draw attention to the word. This is usually the case when the idea expressed is already in play. See Unit 1 Explanation.

iii) No. Dave presents 'give' as a new idea at this point. Dave and Gill have probably mentioned Claire and the fact that it is her birthday or some special occasion but this is the point at which the idea of giving her something is introduced.

1.3 If necessary, play this part several times, and deal with the two halves separately.
Play the first half and ensure the students can hear the $\vee\!\!\nearrow$ movement beginning on 'reading' before concentrating on the $\searrow$ movement which begins on 'book'.

ANSWERS

i)   The pitch movements are: 'reading' $\vee$
                              'book' $\searrow$

ii) Yes. Gill assumes that Dave knows Claire likes reading; she believes it is knowledge shared by them both at this point.

2 Explanation

This is the first of three units on *tone*. This explanation is crucially important for the students' understanding of what follows in these units. It should be studied carefully here and viewed as reference material for future use.

The tones   The basic meaning distinction of the two tone types is introduced but is kept as simple as possible at this point. As more of the system is learnt in working through the course, these basics will be refined and extended.

The 'intonation contour displays', which were produced from the recording on a sonograph, clearly show the main pitch movements. Draw the students' attention to the evidence here that the TONE *begins* on the TONIC SYLLABLE.

Tone units and tonic syllables   Students will not need to identify tone unit boundaries, as this in itself is not important. What is important to convey here is that the pitch movement *begins* on the tonic syllable (and, in fact, extends across tone unit boundaries).

The transcription   This is kept as simple as possible and includes only what the students will need in order to use and talk about the system.

3 Imitation

Play the recording as many times as the students require, and use the exercise as you feel is most appropriate to your teaching situation. In any case, try to hear students individually at this stage.

Remind them that the pitch movement begins on the tonic syllable. In the examples here the tonic syllables occur late in the tone units, as is usually the case, which means that when the tone units are spoken in isolation (that is, not in their conversational context), the pitch movements seem short.

4 Practice activities

Note: Exercises 4.1 and 4.2 may appear rather repetitive and drill-like. They are designed to follow on from the short imitation section and to provide further controlled practice in producing the two tones. If you feel your students do not need so much of this sort of practice, shorten or select from the exercises.

4.1 This is most suitable for pair work, with students alternating roles. At this stage student B should concentrate on only the second and third tone units in the replies. The introductory 'I'm afraid', 'Sorry', etc., are included to make the conversation more natural.

If necessary, go through the exercise first to check that students can express the clue in brackets more fully. It is important that B has formulated each response before beginning it to avoid producing a series of hesitations whilst trying to put the utterance together.

4.2 This is very similar to the last exercise and can be done in the same way.

The first tone unit of B's response can include repetition of part of what A has said, e.g. 'the sports centre' and 'a film', but if your students can handle the use of tones as required here, ask them to find other ways of expressing what A has just said.

POSSIBLE ANSWERS
i)   I'm going *there* tomorrow.
ii) I'm going *to the cinema* this evening.
iii) We're going *to see her* next Monday.
iv) We *went there* last Saturday.
v)   We *did that* on Thursday.
vi) We stayed in last night – is probably the most natural response. Students may wish to include all the information. In this case, the response would be:
     // ∨↗ We stayed IN // ∨↗ and listened to MUsic //
     // ↘ LAST night //

In this way 4.2 is more challenging than 4.1 and, although very similar in form, can be seen to be progressive.

4.3 This can be done as a class activity or in pairs. In either case, ask the students to mark the transcripts and then decide which question is appropriate.

ANSWERS

i)   // ↘ I met RObert // ∨↗ this MORNing //   (a)
ii) // ∨↗ He TOLD me // ↘ he was in LOVE //   (a)
iii) // ∨↗ She's started to WORRy // ↘ about her eXAMS //   (b)
iv) // ↘ I learned SPANish // ∨↗ at SCHOOL //   (b)

To extend the activity, ask the students to work in pairs and ask each other the (a) and (b) questions, to which they must give the appropriate reply each time.

4.4 Play the recording of the examples and get the students to practise the two different responses.

The activity can be done as pair work, or the students can respond to the recording.

You may like to combine these ways of dealing with it: for (i) and (ii) get them to listen to the recording and mark the tones in pencil before responding, then for (iii) and (iv) work in pairs, responding without marking.

ANSWERS

i)   B: // ↘ I'm going to FRANCE // ∨↗ in APril //
     B: // ∨↗ I'm going to FRANCE // ↘ in APril //

ii) B: // ∨↗ He's taken up SWIMMing // ↘ to keep FIT //
     B: // ↘ He's taken up SWIMMing // ∨↗ to keep FIT //

iii) B: // ∨↗ The firm's head OFFice // ↘ is in LONdon //
     B: // ↘ The firm's head OFFice // ∨↗ is in LONdon //

iv) B: // ↘ He appLIED for uniVERsity // ∨↗ when he KNEW he
         had PASSED //
     B: // ∨↗ He appLIED for uniVERsity // ↘ when he KNEW he
         had PASSED //

5 Communication activity

Give students time to study the maps and information sheet, and help out with the pronunciation of place names.

Make sure the instructions and all parts of the information are understood.

It may be useful to give a demonstration of the kind of thing expected:

B: ↘ I'm THINKing of going to ROchester. ↘ What can I SEE there?
A: ↘ There's a caTHEdral ↘ and a CAstle in ∨↗ ROchester. ↘ And
    there's the DICKens Centre.

B: ↘ Can you TELL me ↘ WHERE I can find a ZOO?
A: ↘ YES. ↘↗ There's a ZOO ↘ near CANterbury.

It is not necessary for B to ask about all the towns and the things he/she wants to see in any particular order. In fact, when the activity is being done simultaneously by several pairs, it is more practical if the pairs are working on different parts of the task.

It is useful, if time is available at the end, to draw the group together to discuss the outcome. The students should be able to identify ↘ and ↘↗ tones used naturally in the activity. But there are different ways of expressing the same idea and students shouldn't be expected to produce unnatural, contrived utterances.

Unit 3   More telling and referring

1   Sensitisation

1.1 Play the recording and ask the students only to listen.

1.2 Play it again as often as the students require.
  i)   Get them to work individually or in pairs, as you or they prefer, and mark the tones on the transcript.

ANSWERS

Lisa: ... HELLO TONy // ↗ DID you go for your INterview yesterday //
Tony: // ↘ HI Lisa // ↘ YES // ↘ I DID //
Lisa: // ↘ HOW did it GO //
Tony: // ↘ All RIGHT // ↗ I THINK //
Lisa: // ↘↗ All RIGHT // ↘↗ You DON'T sound very SURE //

Check the transcript as a class activity.

  ii) Now the students all have the right answers, get them to discuss/ explain the use of the tones in this context in pairs. Try to elicit the following points:

INterview = ↘↗ because Lisa already knew that Tony was going for an interview; they shared this knowledge.
YES and I DID = ↘ because here Tony is telling Lisa what she wanted to know.
HOW did it GO = ↘ because, after checking about the interview, Lisa here introduces the new idea of how it *went*.
Lisa: All RIGHT = ↘↗ because she is referring directly to what Tony has just said.
SURE = ↘↗ because Lisa is referring to the way Tony seems to feel when he says 'All right, I think.' They now share the knowledge that he does not feel sure.

2   Explanation

This explanation builds onto the very simple distinction which was made between the two tone types in the last unit. The idea of referring can be difficult for learners to grasp when there is nothing concrete (that is, in lexical terms) in the preceding discourse to refer to.

Remind the students that speakers make choices in their use of intonation as the conversation develops with each passing moment. What can be referred to is any sort of knowledge or experience which the speakers share (or assume they share) at that point in the conversation.

The three functions listed here are derived from the part of the conversation in section 1 and are not intended to be exhaustive.

3   Imitation

3.1 Students are asked to repeat *both* parts. This is to give them the opportunity to practise 'All right' spoken with both tones in a meaningful context.

3.2 This can be done by asking the students to respond to the recording, as suggested. Alternatively, you may wish to give the students a freer hand by getting them to practise in pairs.

3.3 Get the students to listen the first time. Then, the second time, they listen and repeat both tone units. The object here is: (a) to contextualise the message of the second tone unit, and (b) to give controlled practice of making longer utterances.

4   Practice activities

4.1 There is more than one way of saying what is presented here. The example demonstrates what the students have already heard in context.

Any variations in the intonation choices will have different meanings/interpretations, so encourage the students to keep as close as possible to the example in their production of (i) to (v).

4.2 This exercise is the only one in this unit which does not practise longer stretches of conversation. It is included here as it demonstrates how the speaker's choice of a $\vee$ tone can be used to make a minimal response.

By using the *referring* tone B expresses unwillingness to *tell* A anything. He/she neither gives the detailed information which A requires nor says that he/she doesn't know.

Help the students to appreciate this more delicate application of discourse intonation.

You can extend the exercise by getting the students to use a ＼ tone for B's response and showing how the interactive effect is different. The effect is usually to make the conversation incoherent.

Make sure the students note the last part of the rubric and try to provide other suitable responses, using the same tone. For example, other responses to 'Is he doing his essay?' could be:

B: He doesn't want to be disturbed. *or* He says he can't go out.

4.3 Make sure the students notice that in the example A uses a ＼ tone for RIGHT, but that when B agrees with this part a ＼／ tone is used, before the new idea of DIFFicult is introduced with a ＼ tone.

Give the students time to practise (i) to (v), working in pairs, and encourage them to discuss the exercise.

In (iii) the tonic syllable changes from DIAmonds to LIKES as this is the most natural way of saying it. But, as in other cases, alternative versions are possible, depending on the new information B chooses to add.

This activity can be adapted in a variety of ways. Students can work together in pairs to prepare and then change partners for the practice stage. It can be done as a class activity, with random As and Bs interacting.

4.4 Let the students listen to the example first. Then they can practise it either by responding to the recording or working in pairs before starting the rest of the activity.

The absence of transcription should not present any difficulty and, in fact, can help to reassure students that working with a transcription does not make them dependent on it.

ANSWERS

Model // ＼／ We've seen all the good FILMS // ＼／ and we've been to the THEAtre // ＼／ and to a CONcert // ＼ LET's go to a NIGHTclub //

i) B: // ＼／ Here are the ENvelopes // ＼／ and the STAMPS // ＼ but there wASn't any PAper //

ii) B: // ＼ As you KNOW // ＼／ we've invITed the WHITES // ＼／ and the ROBsons // ＼／ but I ALso // ＼ invited the JENkins //

iii) B: // ∨↗ <u>WELL</u> // ∨↗ we've organised the MUsic // ∨↗ and the <u>DRINKS</u> // ↘ but we HAVEn't got the <u>FOOD</u> yet //

iv) B: // ∨↗ We've got <u>AP</u>ples // ∨↗ and <u>PEARS</u> // ∨↗ and <u>PEACH</u>es // ↘ we OUGHT to get some <u>O</u>ranges //

v) B: // ↘ It's <u>DIFF</u>icult // ∨↗ we've been to <u>I</u>taly // ∨↗ and <u>GREECE</u> // ∨↗ and <u>AU</u>stria // ↘ HOW do you feel about <u>TUR</u>key //

5 Communication activity

If possible, pair the students by putting together people who do not know each other very well or who don't see each other much out of the classroom.

1 Students work together and put in their diaries the times they are both occupied with the same things, e.g. classes, organised activities.

2 Now ask them to work individually and to ensure that their partners do not see what they write in their diaries. This is where the information gap is created. Encourage them to leave a few spaces free.

3 The students try to make arrangements by asking questions, e.g.

A: Can we meet for a cup of coffee on Monday?
B: Oh, sorry. ↘ I'm going swimming ∨↗ on Monday.
A: Would you like to go to the cinema to see 'XYZ'?
B: Yes. ↘ What about Friday?
A: ∨↗ I can't make it on Friday. ↘ I'm going to a party. Are you free on Saturday?

Check that they use a ∨↗ tone to *refer* to a time already mentioned. If you find they finish quickly, ask them to find another partner and do part 3 again.

Unit 4 Revision and practice

1 Conversation

1.1 Play the whole conversation once and get the students to discuss with each other the answers to the comprehension questions. If it is necessary, play the recording a second time.

ANSWERS
   i)   Samantha has told Lisa that she has received a dozen red roses from an anonymous admirer.
   ii) John explains that the red roses mean 'He's in love with her'. It may be necessary to check that students from some cultural backgrounds have got the point.
   iii) The two different meanings of 'poor':
        a) The one Lisa gives it here: to be pitied.
        b) The one John gives it here: to have less than is really necessary, e.g. money.

1.2 Play the recording as often as the students require and let them attempt the task without your help.
   i)   They should be able to tell you that the phrase 'a dozen roses' occurs three times.
        As they give you this information write the phrases up on the black/whiteboard in the order they occur in the conversation:
        a DOZen ROSes
        a dozen ROSes
        a DOZen roses
   ii) Now get the students to explain why particular word(s) are highlighted at that point in the conversation.
        a DOZen ROSes – When Lisa first tells John, she wants him to notice what and how many.
        a dozen ROSes – At this point John knows she got a dozen but he's not sure what.
        a DOZen roses – At this point John has just mentioned roses. Now Lisa wants to emphasise how many.
   iii) Get the students to practise saying the phrase in the three different ways by asking them at random:

What did she get?
How many roses?
A dozen what?

1.3 Repeat as for 1.2.
   i) The phrase 'He's in love with her' occurs twice. When the students tell you this write up:
   He's in LOVE with her
   HE'S in love with HER
   ii) Explanations:
   He's in LOVE with her – John is explaining that sending red roses means more than being 'just keen'. It means being *in love*, so now he highlights this information.
   HE'S in love with HER – The idea of 'being in love' is not questioned here. What's important is who is in love with whom.
   iii) Get the students to say the phrases in response to:
   How does he feel about her?
   Who's in love with whom?
   iv) There are also repetitions of 'I KNOW' and 'POOR GUY', but no change in the distribution of prominence with these.

If you feel it is a suitable activity for your group, suggest the students go on to read the dialogue in pairs.

2 Practice activity

This activity revises and extends the work done in Unit 2, 4.3.
   In each case play the recording and ask the students to mark the tones in on their transcripts and decide which is the appropriate question.
   Then, for each part of the activity get them to ask the other question and make the appropriate response – by inverting the ↘ and ∨↗ tones.
   To further extend the activity the students can work in pairs and ask each other all the questions, making a suitable response each time by placing the telling and referring tones in the appropriate part of the utterance.

ANSWERS TO THE RECORDING
i)   // ∨↗ When we've finished LUNCH // ↘ we'll look at the PHOtos // (b)
ii) // ∨↗ Your use of intoNAtion // ↘ can change the MEANing // (b)
iii) // ↘ The hoTEL // ∨↗ was very GOOD // (a)
iv) // ↘ You can GO // ∨↗ if you've FINished // (a)

3   Conversation

3.1 First ask the students to listen to the whole of the conversation between Lisa and Tony. It includes the short part they heard in Unit 3. They should attempt the comprehension questions after hearing it only once.

ANSWERS

i) Tony is worried that he has spoiled his chances of getting the job he wanted because he was not wearing suitable clothes at the interview.

ii) Yes. She tells Tony, 'I'm sure you needn't worry', before she hears he wore jeans. But not everyone may agree with this answer – in which case the question could promote valuable discussion.

3.2 Play the second part as often as is required, if necessary breaking it down into sections. The turn-taking provides convenient breaks.

ANSWERS

Tony: // ↘ I MEAN // ↗ I MANaged to answer all the QUESTions // ↗ and I THINK I said the right THINGS // ↘ but I DON'T think // ↘ I wore the right CLOTHES //

Lisa: // ↘ WELL // ↗ there's NO point in WORRying about it // ↗ what's DONE // ↘ is DONE //

Tony: // ↘ YES Lisa // ↘ I KNOW // ↗ there's NOTHing I can DO about it // ↘ of COURSE // ↗ I CAN'T CHANGE anything // ↘ but I CAN'T help THINKing about it //

Possible explanations:

Tony – He uses ↗ in the second and third tone units because he sees answering 'all the questions' and saying 'the right things' as shared knowledge of what is meant by an interview having gone 'all right'.

– He uses ↘ in the fifth tone unit because when he *tells* Lisa about not wearing the right clothes he does not expect her to have anticipated this.

Lisa   – She uses ↗ to refer to what they both know: that Tony is worrying about it. (Students are not asked to explain the use of the two tones for 'What's done is done', but it may draw comment. Lisa uses a ↗ first as she *refers* to what they now both know has been done. By using ↘ next she is *telling* him he can't undo it.)

Tony – When he uses ∨↗ in the third tone unit he is referring to what Lisa has just said.
– In the fifth tone unit he uses ∨↗ to refer to the same thing.
– He uses a ↘ tone to tell Lisa something he thinks she doesn't know. Perhaps he feels that she doesn't know that he is the sort of person who would worry about things.

3.3 Do the same as before. Alternatively, do this part as a class activity if you feel enough time has been spent on pair work.

ANSWERS
Lisa: // ↘ I'm <u>SURE</u> // ∨↗ you needn't <u>WORRY</u> // ↘ what <u>DID</u> you wear // ↘ <u>AN</u>yway //
Tony: // ↘ I <u>HAD</u> to put my <u>JEANS</u> on //
Lisa: // ∨↗ Your <u>JEANS</u> // ↘ OH I <u>SEE</u> //
Tony: // ∨↗ But I wore a <u>TIE</u> //
Lisa: // ∨↗ <u>NE</u>ver <u>MIND</u> // ∨↗ you <u>SAID</u> the right things // ↘ <u>AN</u>yway //

Possible explanations:
Lisa   – She uses a ↘ tone in the third tone unit to indicate that the information will be new to her.
Tony – He uses a ↘ tone because he is telling Lisa something completely new to her.
Lisa   – She uses ∨↗ for jeans, referring directly to what he has just said.
Tony – He uses ∨↗ for tie because he presents this as something they both associate with interview clothing. At this point Tony seeks to establish a sense of solidarity with Lisa since he fears he has lost some credibility.
Lisa   – She uses ∨↗ for 'said' because she refers to what Tony told her earlier in the conversation.

4   Dialogue reading

This activity is designed to give students the opportunity to consolidate all that has been covered in the first three units of the course.

Get them to work in pairs and first discuss the use of highlighting and ↘ and ∨↗ tones in the dialogue before reading it aloud.

The recorded version is not intended to represent the only, or even the best, way of performing it. Students may be able to recognise and discuss differences in their own presentations and where their own differ from the recording.

Get students to record their reading if possible.

Unit 5 Roles and status of speakers

The title

First discuss with the students the difference in meaning of 'role' and 'status'.

role: part played by someone. This is not limited to character acting in plays, but refers to the way a person behaves in a particular social setting. By doing what is thought to be appropriate, usual or customary a person plays a role.

status: social or professional position, often used relative to others. We talk about 'high' and 'low' status.

1 Sensitisation

1.1 Ask the students to read the two questions and then listen to the conversation with these questions in mind.

1.2 Play the recording as often as you feel is necessary, and break the conversation into chunks which are convenient for the students to handle.

i) Get the students to work individually or in pairs and to mark in the tones on their transcripts.

ANSWERS

Lisa: // ↘ But TOny // ↗ surely you REALised // ↗ everybody would be wearing SUITS // ↗ a job like THAT // ↗ SUCH a good SALary // ↗ with SO much responsiBILity // ↘ you OUGHT to have known BETTer than to wear jeans //

Tony: // ↘ Don't reMIND me // ↘↗ I KNOW it was STUpid //

Lisa: // ↘ Well WHAT was the PROBlem // ↘ I KNOW // ↘↗ you've GOT a suit //

Tony: // ↘ Oh, YES // ↘↗ I've GOT one // ↘ it was at the CLEANer's //

Lisa: // ↗ It was WHERE //

Tony: // ↘ At the CLEANer's // ↘ it still IS //

30

ii) If they are working in pairs, each pair can compare with another pair, or individuals can form different pairs. Then check the transcription as a class activity.

iii) This is explained in section 2, so try to make sure that the students do not look forward in their books. It should be possible to elicit the main point: that the effect of the ⟋ tone is to make the speaker sound dominant.

If students make suggestions such as: Lisa is criticising or reprimanding Tony, you can develop this in such a way that they can see that it amounts to the same as feeling dominant.

The earlier discussion about the title of the unit will have opened their minds to thinking along the right lines.

Draw the students' attention to the fact that Lisa also uses the ⟍⟋ tone. It is important that they see that a speaker who has chosen to use the ⟋ tone does not necessarily choose it every time he/she uses a referring tone in that part of the conversation.

2 Explanation

The first part of the Explanation states what you aimed to elicit in 1.2(iii). It is important that the students appreciate first of all that the rising tone (termed r+ by Brazil) is used by speakers in informal conversation. In this case, the social implication is that the speaker who uses it is claiming dominance at that point.

Lisa uses the rising tone when she refers to things she expected Tony to know or remember. This can be explained by saying she is being forceful about what is (or she feels should be) shared knowledge for both of them.

What is said in the Student's Book about the natural conversational superiority of speakers relating to their status or occupational role has not been demonstrated in the conversation, but it is not difficult for the students to understand.

Make sure the students appreciate that this does not mean that dominant speakers always use a ⟋ rather than a ⟍⟋ tone. The point is that the speaker in the dominant position has the choice, whereas the other speaker does not have the same choice, and by using it inappropriately would risk sounding rude.

It may be useful to add here that native speakers can more easily make allowances for non-native speakers' inaccurate use of grammar and vocabulary than for inappropriate intonation. Furthermore, native speakers are usually able to say what is incorrect about grammar and vocabulary, but in the case of intonation they cannot usually explain what is wrong. However, they cannot help responding to the effect.

3   Imitation

Some students tend to worry about imitating this tone because they feel the rise to a high pitch is unnatural for them.

This can be the case if, by anticipating the rise, they begin at too high a level. If this seems to be happening, suggest they begin at a lower level.

Another problem can be that students do not wait for the tonic syllable before beginning the rise, but try to make the movement extend from earlier in the tone unit. In this case, remind them of what they have already learnt about the pitch movement *beginning* on the tonic syllable.

4   Practice activities

4.1 The addition of the fourth line of the dialogue using a $\vee\!\!\nearrow$ tone makes the exercise more difficult. However, Imitation activity 3.2 should have helped to prepare for this.

Make sure the students change roles, taking A and B, as they work through the activity. Try to monitor and check their production carefully as they may not be able to assess their own accuracy, even when they hear their own compared with the recorded versions.

4.2 You may feel this is quite challenging for your students, so, if they have any difficulty, give them the opportunity to practise the first dialogue by listening to the recording first and then imitating.

Encourage discussion about the difference in effect of the responses here and in 4.1.

4.3 You can get the students to prepare this exercise in pairs and then take it in turns to read the utterances. But, since the exercise is not in dialogue form, you may prefer to do it in some other way.

When the students have worked through both parts, extend the exercise by asking them to go back to the beginning and work through again, this time inverting the tone units in each case. A slight adjustment to the wording is necessary in the first one:

// $\searrow$ Pour the WAter on the TEA // $\nearrow$ as SOON as it BOILS //

4.4 It should not be difficult for the students to come to the conclusions that the dominant roles should be played by the doctor and the bank manager. This final practice activity should be dealt with as a fairly free exercise: encourage the students to experiment with the tones as they practise.

5 Communication activity

First discuss the newspaper advertisement with the class. Draw attention to the word economy and abbreviations: refs = references and tel = telephone.

It may be necessary to indicate that Devon is a county in the south west of England.

Monitor the activity, listening for the appropriate use of both ↗ and ∨ tones.

It is important that student A chooses to use some ↗ tones, but it is even more important that student B does not use them unawares.

Remind student A about the last part of the activity. He/she has to initiate making an appointment if he/she decides that student B is suitable.

Unit 6 Low Key information

The title

First discuss 'low key', a term now in general use which usually means: not being the main focus of attention. Some students may be familiar with it.

Explain the term and give examples of its use, e.g.

– Although I think it's very important, I'm afraid he's being very low key about the whole business.
– The school has a very low key approach to the arts and makes science its most favoured subject.

Low Key will be used in this unit in a special way relating to intonation, but this more general meaning is a useful introduction.

1 Sensitisation

1.1 Ask the students to read the three comprehension questions and keep them in mind when listening to the recording. It may be necessary to play it two or three times and to pause so that the students can get the examples for (ii).

ANSWERS
i)   Because it is a very complicated subject.
ii) Body movements, gestures, facial expressions, 'shadow moves' which go across features and eye movements.
iii) Although it is largely subconscious, we can control it and use it to our advantage – so *yes*.

1.2 The transcription indicates the changes in pitch level, so the students can hear and see what is meant by 'spoken at a low pitch level' as they listen to the recording.

i) The connection between what is said in Low Key and the
and ii) immediate context in Mid Key is fully explained in section 2, so try to elicit the information from the students before they look forward.

The connection between 'I'm sorry to say' and 'final programme' is that 'I'm sorry to say' is something the speaker says
to himself and does not add anything to the main idea of
'final'.

'Thank you for coming' and 'good of you to give us your
time' have the same sort of connection – one does not add anything to the meaning of the other. The sameness of meaning
here is that they both express the interviewer's gratefulness.

1.3 Play the whole of 1.1 again and ask the students to indicate other
instances of Low Key. These are shown in the transcription below
with underlining. This is for your convenience at this point and is
not a normal transcription convention.

ANSWERS

Int.: We have with us this ↓ AFTernoon ↑ for this sixth and

I'm ↓ SORRy to SAY ↑ final programme in the series –
Professor King, who is Professor of Psychology at Towns-
ford University. Thanks for coming, Professor, ↓ GOOD of

you to give us your TIME. ↑ You've made a special study,

I understand, of a subject which I ↓ KNOW I'm RIGHT in

saying ↑ has a special fascination for all of us, ↓ BODy

LANguage.

P.K.: Thank you. Yes, yes, a great deal of interest has been gener-
ated recently. But I think I should point out that there's still
much we don't know or understand about this subject.

Int.: Well, perhaps you could tell us in simple terms what it is.
All sorts of things come into people's minds ↓ as I'M SURE
you're aWARE.

P.K.: Yes, but you ask me to give you a definition in simple terms
of something which is in fact really very complicated.

Int.: Well, perhaps if we could begin with some simple facts.

P.K.: Well, I'll try. At its very simplest, and I realise I'm opening myself here to all sorts of criticism, er, body language is non-verbal communication. It includes body movements, gestures, facial expressions, the sort of shadow moves you see flitting across people's features, eye movements — things we all use, whether we're aware of them or not, and respond to in others.

Int.: I see. Well, that's very interesting. And this is all sub-conscious, is it?

P.K.: Yes, to a ↓ LARGE EXTENT ↑ it is. Yes. We can control it and use it, as we very often do, to our own advantage.

Int.: Well, ↓ perHAPS you could TELL me ↑ why do we need it? Why should speakers of, well, for example, the English language . . .

2 Explanation

The dropping of the pitch level of the voice and the fact that it has significance in conversation may be a new idea for students. The explanation is, therefore, kept very simple.

The feature of Key, dealt with in this and the next unit, concerns the choice of pitch level at the first prominent syllable of a tone unit (onset) relative to that of the preceding tone unit.

In choosing Low Key speakers indicate that what is being said at that point amounts to the same thing as what has just been said or, in some cases, what is about to be said. This equivalence of parts of utterances may be something the hearer is already aware of or something not yet known.

The Student's Book outlines two kinds of Low Key information, both of which are demonstrated in the recorded dialogue. The first kind may be described as non-essential information — in that the main meaning of the utterance is not changed by it. To help students appreciate this concept, get them to say the utterances without the Low Key bits and feel the completeness.

The second kind, here called an 'aside', is often more difficult to explain in terms of being equivalent to anything in the immediate

with his family this year. They've got a villa on Ibiza – and they've got a boat. You know how crazy I am about boats. ↓ I love them.

Sue: Mike, that's marvellous – ↓ very good news. ↑ What a wonderful opportunity for you!

Mike: Yes, but it's not that simple.

Sue: What's the problem?

Mike: It's Celia. You see, we've both been saving up like mad – ↓ every penny we could ↑ – to go on a trip together this year.

Sue: Ah, I see. You don't want to disappoint her, of course, ↓ by going alone.

Mike: That's right, ↓ I don't. ↑ She'd be so upset, ↓ naturally. ↑ She's been doing all sorts of jobs in her free time – ↓ evenings and weekends. ↑ She really deserves this holiday. It seems so unfair.

Sue: Look, Mike. First you must tell Celia about your invitation. She'll appreciate your problem. ↓ She's very understanding. ↑ But why don't you tell Miguel about the plans you had already made with Celia. He might even suggest ...

5 Communication activity

Spend some time going through the instructions, making sure the students are quite clear about what they have to do.

Check the amount of time you can give to the exercise and allow at least a third of this for the students to prepare their stories, working individually at this point. The telling of the stories should be as uninterrupted as possible. It is important that they are recorded. 4 and 5 can be worked as extensively as you wish. To extend the activity further, students can use the outline of their partner's story and add Low Key bits to make it as funny/different as possible.

Unit 7   Contrasts

The title

Discuss the word 'contrast' to check that the students all know its meaning as it is generally used:
As a noun it means 'something being noticeably different from something else', and the word accent is on the first syllable.
As a verb it means 'to show a noticeable difference with something else', and the accent is on the second syllable.
In some contexts it has the added dimension of meaning 'different from what was expected', which is particularly relevant to its use in this unit. This will become clear to the students when they reach section 2.
   Try to elicit or introduce some examples of the general use of 'contrast' in a variety of contexts.

1   Sensitisation

1.1 Get the students to read the two comprehension questions and to keep them in mind as they listen to the recording. You may feel it is necessary to play the whole or part of the conversation a second time.
   Note: Before the students listen, tell them that the word 'garage' is commonly used to mean the place where a car is repaired, as well as car-storage at home.

ANSWERS
   i) Tony is fed up because his car has turned out to be unreliable. It often has to go to the garage for repairs, which is where it is as he is speaking.
   ii) The repairs may not be finished by the next weekend, and Tony has an arrangement with Samantha, which is obviously 'really important'.

1.2 The transcription indicates the shifts to a raised level of pitch so that the students can appreciate what is meant.

i) The connection is fully explained in section 2, so try to
and ii) elicit the information from the students before they look
forward.

1 'It was fantastic' contrasts with what John has assumed, i.e. 'a huge success'. Pat implies that this is not an adequate way of describing the experience and expresses it in another – stronger – way.

2 John: 'Hey, look' – meaning that what Pat will see is different from what she would expect.

3 Tony: 'Oh, hello, John.' The meeting is contrary to his expectations.

4 Tony: 'I thought you were in Paris.' This is in contrast to what I actually see, i.e. you are here.

5 Pat: 'Well, I was.' The use of the past tense here contrasts with the present situation, i.e. *now* it's different.

6 Pat: 'Oh, Tony. It's a lovely little car.' This is in strong contrast to what Tony has just said: he's obviously very disillusioned about it.

All of the above are examples of some kind of contrastive meaning.

1.3 The transcript is supplied here because there are too many examples of raised pitch for the students to indicate without interrupting the flow of the conversation. Get them to use vertical arrows (the ↑ is more important) to mark on their transcripts the places where the rises in pitch occur, *as they listen.*

Let them discuss in pairs before checking as a class activity – if you have time.

As in Unit 6, underlining has been used for your convenience but it is not a transcription convention.

ANSWERS

Pat: But you were so <u>PLEASED with it</u> . . .

Tony: Oh, yes, I WAS. It was <u>JUST what I'd DREAMED of.</u>
A BIT OLD – but in <u>MARvellous con</u>DITion.
AND it was very <u>CHEAP</u>.

John: EXACTly. I reMEMber. I TOLD you at the TIME I was a bit susPICious. But you didn't LISten.

Tony: YES, I <u>DID. I</u> THOUGHT I was <u>LUCKy for once.</u>

Pat: You <u>WERE lucky, Tony.</u> LAST time I saw you, you said it was so re<u>LIable.</u>

Tony: Well, <u>YES</u>. It SEEMED reLIable. For a MONTH or so.
But since THEN it's been at the GArage more than
on the <u>ROAD</u>.

John: So, WHERE is it NOW?

Tony: At the CENtral GArage. I'm HOping to pick it UP first thing
toMORROW.

John: They're exPENsive THERE.

Tony: <u>ACTually, they're</u> NOT. But they're not efFICient, EIther! It
was supPOSED to be ready on <u>MONday</u>.

Pat: <u>MONday! But tomorrow's THURSday.</u> COME ON, CHEER UP,
Tony. You'll <u>HAVE it for the week</u>END.

Tony: Not necessARily. Every time I GO or RING they've found
something <u>ELSE that needs</u> DOing. <u>LAST weekend was</u>
<u>bad e</u>NOUGH without it. But <u>THIS weekend is REALly</u>
<u>important.</u> SaMANtha said ...

2   Explanation

Go through the Explanation with the students to make sure they understand it.

The idea of pitch level variation having significance was introduced in Unit 6, so the students will probably be more receptive to this now.

As with Low Key, the change in pitch level to High Key takes place at the onset and is relative to the pitch level of the onset in the preceding tone unit.

The Student's Book outlines three kinds of contrast and uses examples taken from the conversation they have heard. It is useful here to go through the other examples they found in 1.3 and put them into the categories.

1 Pat: 'pleased with it'   (i)
2 Tony: 'just what I'd dreamed of'   (iii)
3 Tony: 'marvellous condition'   (i)
4 Tony: 'lucky for once'   (i)
5 Pat: 'were lucky, Tony'   (ii)
6 Pat: 'reliable'   (i)
7 Tony: 'Well, yes'   (iii)

8 Tony: 'on the road' (i)
9 Tony: 'Actually, they're not' (ii)
10 Tony: 'on Monday' (i)
11 Pat: 'Monday! But tomorrow's Thursday' (i)
12 Pat: 'You'll have it for the weekend' (i)
13 Tony: 'something else that needs ...' (i)
14 Tony: 'Last weekend was bad enough' (i)
15 Tony: 'But this weekend is really important' (i)

Again, remind students that the lifting of the pitch level operates independently of pitch movement (tone), which they practised in Units 2–5.

3 Imitation

Remind the students that they should repeat only the second speaker's part. For this reason the High Key is transcribed.

English has a fairly wide pitch range, and some students may resist going as high as native speakers do. They may need your encouragement to lift the pitch further. Once they are conscious of it, students will notice that the most 'masculine' male native speakers use a very high pitch sometimes.

Insist on accuracy.

4 Practice activities

4.1 Get the students to work in pairs and alternate roles. Give them a little time to prepare the exercise before asking them to do the productive work.

Alternatively, they can prepare the responses and then respond to the recording.

To extend the exercise, get the students to work in pairs and produce both printed responses, appropriately in High or Mid Key. In fact, if the speaker intends to be very enthusiastic, both responses can be said in High Key, since the alternative can become a 'strong agreement'.

ANSWERS
High Key would normally be used for:
i) b   iv) a
ii) a   v) a
iii) b

4.2 Make sure the students first repeat the example correctly.

... but the hotel was ^{AW}ful.

Give the students time to prepare the utterances first and, if they are working in pairs, to experiment a bit. This is the transcript of the recorded version. The prominent syllables are not transcribed except for those where the High Key choice is made.

i)   ... to help me but he ^{WOULD}n't.

ii) ... but created a^{NOTH}er.

iii) ... and they sent a ^{FIRE} engine.

iv) ... but they were ^{TERR}ible.

4.3 Go through the pictures if you think the students will have any problems explaining them. Discuss them together. Working in pairs, the students decide how to complete the statements and then practise them, assigning High Key. Possible responses are given below; note that prominence and other intonational features are not transcribed in the first part of the utterances.

i)   She went to buy a bicycle and came back with a ^{SPORTS} car.

ii) He wanted to work in the library but it was ^{CLOSED}.

iii) He went to an Indian restaurant and ordered a ^{HAM}burger.

iv) The old ladies wanted to play ^{FOOT}ball.

v)   He needs to lose weight and he eats cakes ^{and SWEETS}.

When the students practise reading they should be able to use High and Mid Key appropriately and without hesitating.

4.4 How you deal with this activity will depend very much on your teaching situation.

Use part of it, at least, for pair work.

If you prefer, do the first section as a class activity. Encourage the students to discuss their decisions to use High Key in the instances they choose.

If possible, let them record themselves and then tell you how they rate their own performance.

Get them to compare their own versions with the recorded one, but remind them that there are various ways of reading the dialogue to make it plausible.

Transcription of recorded version showing moves to High Key only

Section 1

A: So, I hope you're packed and ready to leave.

  B: Yes, yes. I'm packed, but not quite ready. I can't find my passport.

  A: Your ↑ passport? That's the one thing you ↑ mustn't leave behind.

  B: I know. I ↑ haven't lost it. I've packed it and I can't remember which bag it's in. Oh dear.

  A: Well, you'll have to find it at the airport. Come on.

Section 2

  A: Come on. The taxi's waiting.

  B: ↑ Did you say taxi? ↑ I thought we were going in your ↑ car.

  A: Yes, well, I had planned to. But I'll explain later. You've got to be there in an hour.

  B: ↑ Not an hour. The plane doesn't leave for ↑ two hours. ↑ Anyway, I'm ready now. We can go.

  A: Now – you're taking just one case. Is that right?

  B: No, there's one in the hall as well.

  A: Gosh! What a lot of stuff! You're taking enough for a month, instead of a week.

  B: Well, you ↑ can't depend on the weather. It might be ↑ cold.

  A: It's never cold in Tenerife. ↑ Certainly not in May. Come on. We really must go.

Section 3

  B: ↑ Right. We're ready. We've got the bags. I'm ↑ sure there's no need to rush.

  A: There is. I asked the taxi driver to wait two minutes – not twenty.

  B: Look, I'm supposed to be going away to ↑ relax. You're making me ↑ nervous.

  A: Well, I ↑ want you to relax on holiday. But you can't relax yet.

  B: O ↑ K, O ↑ K, I ↑ promise not to relax! At least not until we get to the airport and I find my passport. Then there will be something ↑ else to worry about I suppose.

  A: Maybe not for you. But I don't know how I'm going to get back.

5   Communication activity

First, let the students study their information and help them with anything they do not understand.

Make sure the instructions are clear to them and point out that they must *ask* and *answer* questions.

Either demonstrate the examples, working with a student yourself, or get a pair of students to do so. The idea of the activity is that the students ask their partners questions assuming they did similar things. But, as they did very different things, their expectations are not met, and the partners give contrasting information – for which High Key is used.

You may have to check that each person is getting an opportunity to ask questions. Check also that they do not offer information before they are asked. If they can handle the information well, suggest that the students add some details of their own.

Unit 8 Revision and practice

1 Conversation

1.1 Play the recording through once and ask the students to attempt the question.

The main things which went wrong for Tony are:
- He took his suit to be cleaned and asked Samantha to pick it up for him.
- She was given the wrong one (but, of course, she didn't realise it).
- When Tony saw the suit he knew it wasn't his and went back to the shop to change it. But the shop had already closed.
- He couldn't wear his suit for the interview because it was still at the cleaner's.

If the students have not been able to pick up most of these points, play the last part (from 'Well, what happened?') again.

1.2 The students can work individually or in pairs. In most cases it will be necessary to break this part of the conversation into two parts. Play the recording as often as the students require.

Get the students to compare their transcripts with a partner or another pair. Then check them as a class activity.

ANSWERS

Lisa: // ↘ You're HOPEless // ↗ here you ARE // ↗ with the CHANCE of a LIFEtime // ↗ to get exACTly the job you WANT // ↗ you have ALL the right qualifiCAtions // ↗ a LOT of exPERIence // ↗ NO family TIES // ↘↗ and when the DAY of the interview aRRIVES // ↘↗ YOU'RE in the INterview room // ↘ and your SUIT'S in the CLEANer's //

Tony: // ↘ I KNOW // ↘ I KNOW //

Lisa: // ↘ WELL // ↘ WHAT HAPpened // ↗ did you forGET to GO for it // ↗ lose your TICket // ↘ or WHAT //

Tony: // ↘ NO // ↘↗ but I ASKED SaMANtha // ↘ to pick it UP for me // ↘ and they GAVE her the wrong ONE // ↘↗ by the time I got BACK to the SHOP // ↘ it was CLOSED //

2   Practice activities

2.1 Give the students plenty of time to prepare this. It is a difficult exercise.

Try to monitor all the students before they make their recording.

It is very valuable if students can make a recording and then compare it with the original – where Tony uses ∨ tones.

Make sure they have alternated roles so that every student has had the opportunity to practise the changing of the tones from ∨ to ↗.

2.2 This is the same sort of activity as 2.1 but is in reverse. Do it in the same way, this time monitoring closely to check that 'Lisa' is able to change ↗ tones to ∨. Again, emphasise the value of comparing the students' recordings with the original.

3   Conversation

3.1 The students listen to the whole of the conversation between Pat and Lisa and then attempt the comprehension questions. If they have any difficulty with the questions you may wish to play the relevant parts of the recording again.

ANSWERS

i) The actual place Pat has visited is never mentioned, but we know it is a great fashion centre because she says she has been there to visit the big fashion houses. She obviously works in the fashion industry or 'rag trade' and has been to find out about the next season's fashions for the purposes of dress designing or selling, etc. Students can discuss further along these lines and make suggestions as to where she might have been: Paris, Rome, etc.

ii) She has brought back only a few cheap things that 'took her eye'. She feels that these will disappoint Lisa who is obviously expecting something more sophisticated.

3.2 Play Section 1 of the recording as often as the students require. If the instructions in the Student's Book are followed they will work individually to mark in the Low Key, before comparing their work with a partner.

However, you may feel it is preferable for the students to work in pairs to decide on how to mark the transcript, and then the pairs can do (i) together, i.e. discuss and compare with another pair.

ii) This is probably best done as pair work, followed by class dis
cussion. In each case the Low Key part is equivalent in meaning to
something which the same speaker has just said. Remind students
of what they learnt in Unit 6. Each instance provides valuable discussion material.

ANSWERS

Section 1

Lisa: It WON'T be long before we're BACK, Pat; there's ↓ NOT

much on the ROAD. ↑ HOW ARE you ↓ ANyway?

Pat: FINE, THANKS. ↓ NOW the FLIGHT'S over. It's ↑ REALly

GOOD of you to come out so LATE, Lisa. I'm SORRY you had

to wait so LONG; you ↓ MUST have been here an HOUR.

Lisa: DON'T WORRY. It ↓ WASn't YOUR fault. ↑ ANyway, I BROUGHT

a good BOOK. I always DO, in CASE there's a deLAY. We KNEW

the plane had LEFT late. They ↓ MADE an anNOUNCEment.

3.3 If your teaching situation is appropriate, the next two sections can
be worked through in the same way as the first. You may like to
introduce some variety by varying the way it is done, in terms of
individual/pair/group/class work.

The three sections constitute a lot of transcribing and it is not
necessary to do them all. Omit as you feel suitable to cut down on
time spent on this activity.

ANSWERS

Section 2

Pat: WELL, I'm so glad you DID come. There AREn't any TRAINS

now – ↓ NOT at THIS hour.

Lisa: I'm REALly looking FORWARD to HEARing about your TRIP. It

seems ↓ Ages since you WENT. ↑ WHEN WAS it?

Pat: ONly a couple of WEEKS ago. At the ↓ beGINNing of the
MONTH. ↑ But I aGREE – it ↓ DOES seem ages. ↑ But I've
DONE such a LOT in that time, met so many PEOple ...

Lisa: Was it ALL business, or DID you find time for PLEAsure?

Pat: I spent MOST of the time WORKing – well, every MORNing and
afterNOON.

Section 3

Lisa: You DIDn't get the CHANCE to go to any GALLeries or
muSEums – ↓ WORKing every DAY.

Pat: NO, I DIDn't. Not THIS time. But it WAS a BUsiness trip; I
DIDn't exPECT to. I was VIsiting the big FASHion houses and
THAT sort of thing, which I ↓ CAN'T do in LONdon.

Lisa: It sounds SO exCITing – you ↓ ARE LUCky. Did you ↑ BUY
anything? I'd LOVE to SEE what's in those SUITcases.

Pat: I THINK you MIGHT be disappOINTed, Lisa. NO desIGNer
clothes, you know. ↓ JUST a few CHEAP things that ↑ TOOK
my EYE.

4 Practice activities

4.1 This first exercise concentrates on High Key. You may wish to tell
your students this – depending on how well you think they can cope
with it. Not all the utterances contain High Key, however, and you
may wish to tell the students this before they begin.

It can be done as a class activity or in pairs. Students discuss the
two statements and decide which one is appropriate.

To extend the activity, get the students to say the utterance they
heard in a way which corresponds to the meaning of the other
statement.

ANSWERS

i) b He asked her and she <u>refused</u>.

ii) b They've gone on holiday, to India.

iii) a The <u>South of</u> France had snow too.

iv) b She brought her <u>children with her.</u>

v) b She put it in the washing machine.

Note that (ii) and (v) do not contain High Key.

4.2 This exercise is similar to 4.1 but concentrates on Low Key. Do it in the same way.

It is true that other intonational choices are significant in giving the utterances here the two possible meanings. For example, in (ii), (iv) and (v) the choice of two tonic syllables is significant; the utterance would be spoken as one tone unit to give it the alternative meaning. However, the choice of Low Key is also a deciding factor and the students' skill in recognising it is practised.

ANSWERS

i) a He applied for the job and <u>got it.</u>

ii) b Read the instructions which are <u>important.</u>

iii) b They went part of the way by bus and <u>walked the rest.</u>

iv) a She wants to learn to skate <u>like her friends.</u>

v) a He is speaking to the doctor who has just arrived.

Note that (v) does not contain Low Key.

4.3 Get the students to work in pairs, if possible. They should spend time discussing the two replies to determine which one should contain Low Key information.

In each case the appropriate response will contain information which is clearly non-essential to the main message, e.g. buying an umbrella is a predictable result of going to an umbrella shop, whereas the information after 'greengrocer's' adds to the information B has given A.

Students working in pairs should record themselves and then try to assess their own performance.

ANSWERS
i)   b
ii) a
iii) b
iv) a